HOW I
CHANGED
the WORLD

Susan B. Anthony

WORLD
BOOK

Susan B. Anthony

WORLD
BOOK

World Book, Inc.
180 North LaSalle Street
Suite 900
Chicago, Illinois 60601
USA

For information about other "How I Changed the World" titles, as well as other World Book print and digital publications, please go to **www.worldbook.com**.

For information about other World Book publications, call 1-800-WORLDBK (967-5325).

For information about sales to schools and libraries, call 1-800-975-3250 (United States) or 1-800-837-5365 (Canada).

Library of Congress Cataloging-in-Publication Data for this volume has been applied for.

How I Changed the World
ISBN: 978-0-7166-2278-9 (set, hc.)

Susan B. Anthony
ISBN: 978-0-7166-2279-6 (hc.)
ISBN: 978-0-7166-4393-7 (pf.)

Also available as:
ISBN: 978-0-7166-2285-7 (e-book)

CONTENTS

CHAPTER 1

Life as a Quaker

Family and Early Life

Susan Brownell Anthony was a leader in the women's rights movement. She was also a social reformer who helped to achieve woman suffrage in the United States. As a member of the American Anti-Slavery Society, she believed in the equality of men and women, no matter the color of their skin, and took part in the movement to end slavery in America. In 1851, she met Elizabeth Cady Stanton, another leading figure in the women's rights and abolition movements. The two became lifelong friends. They helped to establish the American Equal Rights Association (AERA) in 1866. At the beginning of her career, Susan was widely ridiculed. She was seen as wanting to destroy the institution of marriage. However, the public's perception of her changed radically during her lifetime. In 1979, she became the first woman to be pictured on U.S. currency.

Susan's father, Daniel Anthony, was a Quaker. Also known as the Religious Society of Friends, the Quakers began as a spiritual movement in the 1600's in England. Their prayer services involved sitting in silence as a kind of meditation as they awaited God's "Inner Light" (presence) to be revealed to them. They dressed in simple, nondescript clothing and stood apart by how they spoke. For example, they would use "thee" and "thou" in place of "you" in their everyday speech. When Daniel married Lucy Read on July 13, 1817, it scandalized the traditional community of Adams, Massachusetts, and embarrassed his family. One reason for this was that Daniel had not sought approval for the marriage from his Quaker congregation. Another reason was that Lucy was not a Quaker. She had grown up and lived among them but remained a lifelong Baptist, though not a practicing one. She often dressed in lively colors, went to parties, and liked to sing, all of which clashed with Quaker practice and beliefs.

Shortly after Daniel and Lucy were married, a delegation of Quaker officials visited their home. They told Daniel that by marrying Lucy, he was guilty of violating the basic beliefs of their faith. When they passed judgment on her husband, Lucy listened from the next room. To the surprise and dismay of the delegation, Daniel did not renounce his marriage to Lucy. He remained loyal and steadfast to his new wife, but he also did his best to make peace with the Quaker community in which they lived. Daniel submitted a formal apology to the Society of Friends for his "misconduct" in marrying a non-Quaker. This did not go over well with Lucy and might be one reason she never became a Quaker. After the Society's reaction to the "scandal" of her marriage to Daniel, Lucy withdrew from the community around her. She refused to accept her husband's way of life. This left Lucy isolated and at times lonely. Women of her day had little say at home or in public, but they had ways of maintaining their dignity. Daniel continued to attend Quaker meetings, but his beliefs gradually became more radical after the confrontation with his traditionalist congregation.

Daniel and Lucy lived with Lucy's parents when they were first married. However, Daniel was busy building a house of their own on farmland that Lucy's

Susan was born in this large, but simple house on Feb. 15, 1820, in Adams, Massachusetts. The house was built by her father, Daniel Anthony, a Quaker.

mother gave to them. When it was finished, the Anthony home was large but extremely simple. In Quaker fashion, there were no decorations, musical instruments, or any other kind of distraction. About a year into their marriage, Daniel and Lucy had their first child—a daughter named Guelma. She was named after the first wife of William Penn, the Quaker founder of Pennsylvania. Unfortunately, Guelma's birth did not bring Lucy out of her social isolation. In fact, having children only seemed to increase it.

It was into this environment that Susan B. Anthony was born on Feb. 15, 1820. The birth of Daniel and Lucy's second child went smoothly. Susan was a strong and healthy baby, and her parents were very happy. Over the next 14 years, five more children were added to the Anthony household. Hannah was born 19 months after Susan. Then came Daniel in 1824, Mary in 1827, Eliza in 1832, and finally Jacob Merritt in 1834. Another child, Anna Eliza, was born in 1833 but did not survive. Daniel and Lucy loved their children and raised them the best way they knew how. Following Quaker tradition, Daniel did not allow toys, games, or music to be a part of their lives. However, he taught all of the children—the boys and the girls— to have discipline, to support themselves, and to believe in their own self-worth. As with everyone else in her life, Lucy remained withdrawn and emotionally distant from her children. Yet, she was devoted to them in her own quiet, modest ways.

While Lucy did her best to find solace in her private world, Daniel decided to give up farm life and try his hand at industry. The power loom was introduced in Waltham, Massachusetts, in 1815, making it possible to mass-produce cotton cloth. Daniel hoped to take advantage of opportunities that came with this invention. He decided to build a cotton mill—the first of many—next to a small brook near his home in Adams. In 1822, it began operations with 20 looms and 23 workers. He depended on Lucy and his children to help support his new business. Lucy took in 11 of his workers as boarders, and Daniel's sister Hannah took in the other 12.

Susan grew up in a home that was bustling with activity, but otherwise her childhood was uneventful. She and her family were working-class people. Much of Susan's daily life was spent doing manual labor.

Only when that work was done was she allowed to play. Each day, she had to help her mother prepare three meals for the family and their boarders and then assist in doing the laundry. In those days, both tasks were considered "women's work." Doing the laundry was a particularly difficult chore. Susan had to carry buckets full of water from a nearby stream all the way to the kitchen so it could be boiled. Years later, Susan claimed it was her ordinary background and the hard work she had to do every day that made it possible for her to be a leader in the women's rights movement.

Such were the normal conditions of the average working-class woman's life in America at that time. This, of course, made a women's rights movement all but impossible. Married women of the day depended on their husbands and lacked the kind of social space necessary to think and act collectively on their own behalf. Only in the 1830's, when women made up 68 percent of the work force in cotton mills, would things begin to change. However, women who worked outside the home were still considered "unladylike." Many more things would have to change before a women's rights movement became possible, but mill-work (along with women's seminaries) was the first step down this long road.

The Move to New York

Daniel's cotton mill proved to be a great success. Known for his Quaker "square dealing," Daniel had a good reputation in the local business community. In 1826, he received a generous offer from John McLean, a judge and cotton manufacturer in New York state. McLean told him that he would put up the money to build a cotton factory if Daniel was willing to relocate. It was an offer Daniel could not refuse. When Susan was about six years old, he moved the family from Adams, Massachusetts, to Battenville, New York. Battenville was a small town near the Battenkill River. It was about 35 miles north of Albany and 10 miles east of the Hudson River in the foothills of the Adirondack Mountains. The town had only a few houses when the Anthony family moved there. Within 10 years, Daniel turned Battenville into a small industrial town and became one of the most important people in the community. Except for the churches and the tavern, most of the town was built by Daniel himself or as a result of his factory.

The Anthony family was doing well in the early 1830's. Daniel would often travel to New York City to sell his wares, but life at home for Lucy and the children changed very little. Long hours of hard work continued to fill their days. Once, however, Daniel agreed to let Susan replace one of his workers who fell ill. She earned three dollars for two weeks of work. Susan was excited at the opportunity. She still did not earn as much as the men who worked in the mill, but it was a break from the dull and monotonous housework to which she was accustomed. When she was 11 years old, Susan asked her father to make one of his weavers, Sally Ann Hyatt, an overseer at the mill. Susan felt that Sally knew more about her job than her own boss. Daniel was firmly against the idea. "It would never do," he said, "to have a woman overseer in the mill." After that, there was no more discussion on the subject. But Susan never forgot what appeared to her to be a clear contradiction between a woman's ability and the social limits placed on her opportunities to apply that ability.

As his business continued to grow rapidly, Daniel decided to expand his holdings. In the spring of 1832, he had a new 15-room house built for his growing family. Lucy was pregnant again, but it remained her duty to

> *Daniel's approach to education, based on his Quaker belief, was that both boys and girls deserved a full education.*

provide food and shelter for the dozen bricklayers
Daniel hired to build their new home. Yet Lucy was so
ill during most of her pregnancy that Susan and her
sisters had to prepare meals and keep the house clean.
In 1834, the Anthony family moved into their new
home. Unfortunately, this happy time was cut short
when Susan's baby sister, Eliza, suddenly died. A few
months later, Lucy gave birth to her last child, Jacob
Merritt.

Initially, the Anthony children attended the
district school in Battenville. One day, however, Susan
came home from school quite upset. She told her
father that her teacher would not teach her long
division because she was a girl. Daniel's approach to

Young Susan urged her father to make one of the women weavers at his mill an overseer. This image shows a woman operating a power loom for weaving cotton in 1840.

education, based on his Quaker belief, was that both boys and girls deserved a full education. After the incident with Susan's teacher, he withdrew his children from the district school and began to home school them. He also provided evening classes for his employees.

In the beginning, Daniel taught these classes himself, but the factory demanded too much of his time. To find a replacement, he inquired at one of the new women's seminaries and hired Mary Perkins to teach in his school. Miss Perkins introduced new teaching methods to the Anthony school. She taught her students to recite poems and to do physical exercises. When she began to teach them music and songs, Daniel put a stop to it. This was one step too far for his Quaker views to accept. He believed that music incited passions, which could have negative effects and distract the students from their pursuit of knowledge.

As a teacher, Miss Perkins held a position that was traditionally reserved for men. Well-educated and independent minded, she offered a new vision of womanhood to Susan and her sisters. When they were old enough, Susan and Guelma followed the example of Miss Perkins and found teaching jobs during the summer months when male teachers left the district schools behind to do farm work. While teaching summer school was more like babysitting, this was the first step toward women teaching in elementary schools. Susan taught her students basic reading and writing skills. Then she would help with the daily chores at home.

Before too long, Susan became aware of the limits placed upon her own education. When Daniel saw how much his daughter loved school and was eager to learn more, he considered enrolling Susan in Deborah Moulson's Female Seminary, a Quaker boarding school in Hamilton, Pennsylvania. Susan's older sister Guelma had gone there and was offered a position as a teaching assistant. Just as Daniel was ready to enroll Susan in the school, however, his business took a plunge from which it would never recover.

Hard Times

The early 1830's were a time of rapid economic development for the United States. Like Daniel Anthony's factory, many new mills and factories that sprang up during those years were very profitable. There was a great deal of optimism in the national economy, but it stood on shaky ground. While the value of property climbed to new heights, it was accompanied by reckless investments. U.S. President Andrew Jackson decided to shut down the Bank of the United States. Failing to understand how banks worked, Jackson disliked and distrusted them. Established in 1816, the charter for the Bank of the United States was up for renewal in 1836. But Jackson refused to renew the bank's charter. His action caused an immediate downward spiral in the economy. The financial crisis that followed became known as the Panic of 1837.

As the economy worsened, Daniel and Lucy began to be careful with their money, but they refused to sacrifice their children's education. By the end of 1837, they had saved enough money to pay the $125 tuition to enroll Susan at Deborah Moulson's seminary. When she joined her older sister there, Susan

When the Panic of 1837 hit, many people blamed President Andrew Jackson. His hat, eyeglasses (under his hat), and pipe with the word "Glory" appear in the sky overhead in this political cartoon reflecting the hard times caused by the financial crisis.

was thrilled at the opportunity that it offered. On the way to Hamilton, Daniel took his two daughters to nearby Philadelphia to do some sightseeing. Susan marveled at the sights of the city. Finally, they arrived at the seminary. When it came time for Daniel to leave, it was a difficult moment for Susan. Overcome with emotion, she said a teary farewell.

Once her father was on his way back to Battenville, Susan had only Guelma for support. She was homesick for weeks. It was more than the usual homesickness that children often go through, however. Susan was now 17, nearly an adult, and found herself experiencing the worst emotional upset of her life. She had always been a serious child. Now she was an intense, passionate young person and desperately missed her family. Forced to enter a social world that was unfamiliar to her, she resisted. Like her mother, Susan withdrew from the people around her and spent long hours writing letters back home.

In time, the intense curriculum of the seminary forced Susan to submerge herself in her studies, and she overcame her depression. She studied arithmetic, algebra, English literature, chemistry, philosophy, and bookkeeping. At a young age, Susan adopted a strategy she would turn to for the rest of her life. She taught herself to channel her strong emotions into her schoolwork. Later in life, Susan's work became the expression of her deepest passions. Deborah Moulson's seminary had a long-lasting effect on Susan. The principles upon which the school had been built were "humility, morality and love of virtue." Deborah Moulson's intention was to instill these values in the girls who studied at the seminary. She also wanted to create a space where they could learn to think and act for themselves outside the home. These were lessons that Susan took to heart.

At the end of Susan's first term in the seminary, her father came to the school to bring his daughters back to Battenville. On the way home, Daniel gave them some bad news. His business was close to bankruptcy. Due to the financial crisis gripping the country, he had been forced to close one factory and most of his mills. Their home in Battenville had also been lost. Consequently, he could no longer keep the two of them in school. Susan was devastated. But she did not understand the full extent of her family's desperate situation until she arrived back home. An auction had been set up to sell everything they owned. In the end, Susan's parents were saved from complete humiliation when Joshua Read, Lucy's brother, stepped in to help. Buying most of their belongings, he made himself the Anthony family's "lenient creditor."

The hard times experienced by the Anthony family meant Susan and her sisters had to look for teaching positions. This would help them to support the family while at the same time continue their education. Susan found work but returned home several months later when her father reopened their home school. Within a few weeks, however, he was forced to close it for good, and the family moved to Hardscrabble, New York. (Hardscrabble was later named Center Falls when Daniel was postmaster there.) Susan did not like the town at all. She described it as a bunch of "brown hovels" with a "broken rough appearance." As the family settled into the new home, Susan worried about what the future might hold. She did not think she would ever be able to go to school again. Yet this, too, proved to be another step on the path toward her career as a leader in the women's rights movement.

The Stirrings of Social Activism

In their new home in Hardscrabble, life went on for the Anthony family. Once again, they took in boarders to make some additional money. The family's financial situation required the older children to support themselves or get married. After a short courtship, Guelma married Aaron McLean. Aaron was the son of Judge McLean, who went on to become a successful businessman in Battenville. Susan decided to look for work. In May 1839, when she was 19 years old, she landed a job as an assistant teacher at Eunice Kenyon's Quaker boarding school in New Rochelle, New York.

Susan really liked her new school, even if it meant being away from her family again. To overcome her loneliness, she wrote Guelma often. However, her sister did not write back as frequently now that she was married. Susan could tell she was losing Guelma, with whom she had always been close, to Guelma's new husband. This hurt Susan's feelings, and she adopted her mother's strategy for dealing with this type of situation. She withdrew from

Guelma emotionally. It was a hard time for both women. When her sister Hannah got married, this pattern repeated itself. As for getting married herself, Susan did not seem interested. None of the men who courted Susan seemed to live up to her intellectual and other standards. Years later, after she had discovered her life's work, Susan made an active choice to remain single.

During this time, Susan began to form her own ideas about politics and the equality of men and women. Once, while she was teaching in New Rochelle, U.S. President Martin Van Buren visited the town on a campaign tour. Nearly every resident in New Rochelle came out to see him. Susan felt the town acted as if "an angelic being had descended from heaven." She was shocked by this. She also learned that her own family had acted in a similar way when Van Buren visited Saratoga Springs. To Susan, the president of the United States was an ordinary man who deserved the basic respect owed to every human being—and nothing more. This was the beginning of Susan's defining belief that no one person was superior to any other person.

By 1845, the Anthony family's financial situation had improved. With some inheritance money from Lucy's father, she and Daniel purchased a farm just outside of Rochester, New York. There, the Anthony family became acquainted with a group of Quaker social reformers. These Quakers had left their traditional congregation because their elders had placed

too many restrictions on their activities. The Anthony farmstead soon became a gathering place for like-minded Quakers who wanted to do something about the injustices they saw in the world. They were often joined by abolitionists from all over the Northeast. William Lloyd Garrison, John Brown, and Frederick Douglass were among the people who visited the farm over the years. A former slave, Frederick Douglass was now a prominent leader in the movement to end slavery in America. During his career, he advised several presidents of the United States. In time, he and Susan became close friends.

The following year, Susan moved to Canajoharie, New York. At the age of 26, she became the headmistress of the girls' department at Canajoharie Academy. Responsible for 20-some girls, Susan was paid a handsome sum of around $100 a year. For the first time in her life, she found herself outside of Quaker influence

The Anthony farmstead near Rochester, New York, became a gathering place for abolitionists, including such prominent leaders as Frederick Douglass (left) and William Lloyd Garrison. In time, Douglass and Susan became close friends.

At age 26, Susan left behind her Quaker habits when she became the headmistress of the girls' department at Canajoharie Academy in 1846. This is a postcard image of the school.

and completely independent. It was something that she very much enjoyed. In Canajoharie, Susan decided to leave behind the Quaker habits of plain speech and dress and began to wear stylish new clothes. Writing home, she told her parents that she was happy with her new life.

Before too long, however, Susan began to feel that being a headmistress no longer offered any challenge. At first, she had been nervous about the prospect of overseeing half of Canajoharie Academy. Now it seemed too easy. Susan told her mother in a letter that she was tired of academics and wanted something more. The only problem was that she did not know what that was. At the time, politics did not really interest Susan and the idea of gaining suffrage, or the power to vote, for the women of the United States did not inspire her. (Due to his Quaker beliefs, Susan's father had never voted.) Nevertheless, the desire in Susan's heart to make the world "a happier and more glorious" place remained strong.

The Path to Social Reform

The Temperance Movement

In 1848, the temperance movement caught Susan's attention. Temperance was a social movement against the drinking of alcoholic beverages that started to sweep the country in the 1820's. Before the end of 1848, Susan helped to form a local chapter of the Daughters of Temperance in Canajoharie. On March 2, 1849, she made her first public speech as the chapter's "presiding sister." In her passionate address, which she delivered to an audience of about 200 people, she called Canajoharie a "hot bed of vice and drunkenness." She told her listeners that lack of self-control with alcohol was at the root of all social and moral decay. She appealed to the women of the town to join in the great cause of "virtue, love and temperance." It was their duty, she said, "to declare themselves on the side of reform." This was a message that Susan would deliver for the rest of her life.

After her speech to the Daughters of Temperance, Susan found herself at a crossroads. She had dedicated more than 10 years of her life to educating children. Now, at 29 years old, she was beginning to feel that she had stumbled upon the means to transform the world around her. That autumn, Susan made a leap of faith and resigned her position at Canajoharie Academy. At her farewell dinner, one of her co-workers praised her as "the smartest woman that is now or ever was in Canajoharie." Shortly afterward, she made her way home to Rochester. Susan offered to help run the Anthony farm while she decided what course to pursue in life. During her tenure at Canajoharie Academy, her father had begun to sell insurance to supplement the family's income. This kept him quite busy, and he was grateful for Susan's help.

Susan kept busy on the farm, but she made time to join the Rochester chapter of the Daughters of Temperance. Once again, she had the chance to demonstrate her natural organizational abilities. She arranged dinners and fairs and traveled to neighboring communities to share with the women there how to do the same thing. In 1850, the national debate on slavery grew in intensity when the United States Congress passed the Fugitive Slave Act, which made slavery a protected institution. Essentially, it deprived runaway slaves of the right to a trial by jury if they were caught in the free Northern States. The law made it a crime to help runaway slaves. Susan's father, however, did everything in his power to help fugitive slaves make their way north to Canada on the underground railroad. Before long, Susan came to believe that the temperance and abolition movements ought to work hand in hand.

In February 1851, Susan spoke at a temperance festival in Rochester. She told her audience that women who lived their lives as slaves in the South deserved

Susan helped form a local chapter of the Daughters of Temperance in Canajoharie, New York. This 1856 Daughters of Temperance poster represents "virtue, love, and temperance."

at least as much sympathy as women who were battered by their drunken husbands in the North. Hearing about her speech, Abigail Kelley Foster, a well-known abolitionist, and her husband, Stephen, came to the Anthony farm to meet with Susan. Abigail Foster immediately sensed Susan's eagerness to do more. She invited her on a weeklong speaking tour and offered to help her become more involved in the abolitionist movement. During their conversation, Abigail Foster made a great impact on Susan. Susan had doubts about what she would have to offer, but she agreed to go on the tour. Despite her organizational skills and deep desire to treat the ills of society, Susan remained doubtful of her own ability to communicate effectively on a larger stage. This would all begin to change later that year when she met Elizabeth Cady Stanton.

Elizabeth Cady Stanton

When Susan first met Elizabeth Cady Stanton, it was an encounter that would change both women's lives forever. Yet, neither of them realized it at the time. In May 1851, Amelia Bloomer, a mutual friend, introduced Susan to Stanton after a lecture given by William Lloyd Garrison in Seneca Falls, New York. Years later, Stanton recalled liking Susan from the start, but it was Susan who stood in awe of the other. More than anyone else, Elizabeth Cady Stanton was responsible for launching the women's rights movement in America. In 1848, she had presented her Declaration of Rights and Sentiments at the Seneca Falls Convention, the first women's rights convention ever held. As the principal author of this landmark declaration, Stanton helped to gain greater equality for women at a time when a woman's traditional role in society was firmly established.

In time, Susan and Elizabeth Stanton became friends and partners in the woman suffrage movement. Little is known about their early friendship. But each woman must have recognized the strengths and special talents that the other possessed. Despite vastly different upbringings, backgrounds, and personalities, Susan and Stanton were propelled into a great struggle for equality that brought them close together in a short amount of time. Stanton, with a husband and four children at home, was in desperate need of someone to help take her message of women's rights to the American people. She soon realized that Susan, with her seemingly endless energy and administrative skills, was the obvious choice. Though Susan remained unsure of her speaking abilities, Stanton convinced her to take up the challenge.

They started with the temperance movement. Susan had been involved for several years now with the Daughters of Temperance. It was the female branch of the Sons of Temperance, a brotherhood of men who promoted temperance. But she had grown tired of working under the clergymen who dominated the women's organization. They controlled both its finances and agenda, and they did not treat Susan and the scores of other women in the movement as equal partners. This annoyed Susan a great deal. Though her commitment was no less than that of the clergymen, these "white orthodox male Saints," as she called them, had no time for her ideas or opinions. In January 1852, Susan was chosen to represent the Rochester chapter of the Sons of Temperance at a statewide convention. She had gathered the required number of petitions calling upon the New York legislature to ban the production and sale of alcohol. No one else had done more than Susan. Her reward was attending the brotherhood's

> *Susan was determined to start her own organization. Calling it the Women's State Temperance Society. . .*

convention. When it came time
for her to address the assembly,
however, the chairman did not let
her speak. He said the women at
the convention had been invited
"to listen and learn," not to speak.
Outraged, Susan and several of
her female associates stormed out
of the hall.

Susan was determined to start
her own organization. Calling it
the Women's State Temperance
Society, it was to be run completely by women, and men would not
be able to vote or hold office in it.
Susan turned to her new friend,
Elizabeth Cady Stanton, and asked her if she would
consider being its first president. Stanton consented
and immediately began to prepare a speech for the
new society's first meeting, which took place on April
20, 1852. Meeting in Rochester's Corinthian Hall, the
Women's State Temperance Society consisted of 500
members—all of them women. Stanton was elected
president, with Susan to serve as secretary.

In her address, Stanton established a radical
agenda and challenged some of the basic beliefs of the
temperance movement. Many of the new society's
members were not prepared for this. The traditional
view in the temperance movement stated that alcohol
was the source of men's unjust use of power over
women. Stanton did not agree. She believed that if all
use of alcohol were somehow stopped, men's oppres-

Susan was in awe of Elizabeth Cady Stanton (above, holding her daughter Harriot) when she first met Stanton in 1851. Stanton was responsible for launching the women's rights movement in America.

sion would continue. To achieve real change, a change in attitude and the law would be required. She suggested that any woman married to an alcoholic should be able to file for divorce. (In the state of New York at the time, the only grounds for divorce were adultery.) Stanton also urged her listeners to help the "poor and suffering" of America, rather than support missions in foreign countries or prop up the "theological aristocracy" (upper class) or organized religion.

After her controversial speech, Stanton returned to Seneca Falls. Once there, she continued to call for woman suffrage. However, she was now expecting her fifth child and was unable to make further public appearances until the baby was born. She therefore called upon Susan to spread their message, leaving her to take the brunt of the opposition's fury. In September, Susan went to Syracuse, New York, and attended her first meeting of the National Women's Rights Convention. She supported Lucretia Mott to be its president and once again took on the role of secretary. Though woman suffrage did not become the focus of Susan's work for several years, this meeting convinced her that the one right women needed most of all—the one necessary to attain all others—was the right to vote.

In June 1853, Susan and Stanton convened the second annual meeting of the Women's State Temperance Society in Rochester. When they did so, their opponents were ready for them. The conservative wing of the society was eager to refocus their efforts on the battle against alcohol and its consumption. With the majority backing them, they altered the constitution and allowed men to vote. In short order, the issues of woman suffrage and changing the divorce laws, both of which were considered scandalous by many delegates, were dropped from the society's agenda. Stanton was also voted out of office. Susan resigned in protest over the way Stanton was treated, despite all the time and energy Susan had put into the organization.

Their first joint campaign established the working style that Susan and Stanton followed during their career together. Over the next half-century, Stanton would provide the foundation for their work and hold the higher office, while Susan would take charge of organizing their day-to-day activities and bringing Stanton's "highest convictions of truth" to wider audiences. While Stanton failed to revolutionize the temperance movement, she accomplished something far more important for women's rights. She empowered Susan to become a tireless champion in the important struggle that lay ahead.

Early Political Action

The winds of change were once again shifting in Susan's life. She had gone from being a teacher of young children to a leader in the temperance movement. After struggles and disappointments in the movement, Susan took some time to reconsider the focus of her life's work. During this time, she remained close to her family. She also maintained a close circle of friends that was almost exclusively female, but work always came first with Susan. After a brief period of rest, she left home with renewed determination. While touring New York state in the summer of 1853, she was disappointed to learn that many of the local temperance societies that she had helped to organize the previous year had all but disappeared. One of the main reasons was a lack of funds. Financially dependent on their husbands, the women of the movement had little money to print leaflets or rent halls for speakers. In 1848, the state of New York passed the Married Women's Property Act—one of the first of its kind—allowing women to inherit money. However, they still had no legal right to the money they earned or any of their husband's money.

Susan realized that nothing was going to change if women had no hope of financial independence. She was determined to address this issue. As she traveled from town to town, she convinced 60 women to help her obtain 6,000 signatures in six weeks' time to call upon the state legislature to expand the Married Women's Property Act. They obtained another 4,000 signatures aimed at securing women the right to vote. Susan then called upon her friend Elizabeth Cady Stanton to help spread the word. In February 1854,

Stanton gave a fiery speech in Albany. Afterward, Susan had 50,000 copies of the address printed up and spread across New York. She also made sure every legislator in the state received one. Nevertheless, both Susan and Stanton knew they faced an uphill battle.

Throughout 1854, Susan kept up the pressure on the New York legislature. She traveled for months at a time, visiting every county in New York. She even traveled during the winter because the harsh weather kept farmers at home and there was little competition from other speakers. Susan drew large crowds almost everywhere she went. Some people came to listen to her simply because of the novelty at the time of hearing a woman speak in public. Others believed in her message and came to hear what she had to say. Susan was also widely covered by the press. Not everyone agreed with what she was fighting for, but most agreed that her arguments were both forceful and eloquent. Susan drove herself so hard that year that she injured her back. At one meeting, she had to be carried in and out of the hall to deliver her address. To make her next speech in a town 17 miles away, she

Elizabeth Cady Stanton gave a fiery speech on women's rights at the State Woman's Rights Convention in Albany, New York. Susan made sure every legislator in the state received a copy like the one above.

had to lie on the seat of a sleigh for the duration of the trip. Susan remained completely devoted to the struggle to achieve equal rights for women.

During the 1850's, Susan also started attending teachers' conventions with mixed success. At her first appearance, she sparked a half-hour debate among the men there about whether a woman should be allowed to speak. Susan won that debate. In 1857, she called for the admission of African American students to New York's public schools and universities. This proposal, however, was soundly defeated. She was verbally attacked by her opponents when she proposed that men and women be educated together at all levels, including at universities.

One of her opponents, Charles Davies, a professor of mathematics at West Point military academy, denounced her ideas about coeducation as "a vast social evil." Susan's resolution was even voted down by most women at the convention that year. Susan often felt isolated and overwhelmed by her opposition, but she kept fighting for what she thought was right. She continued to speak at teachers' conventions for several years. She demanded that women be allowed to hold office in the New York State Teachers' Association, and she insisted that they deserved equal pay for their work.

The American Anti-Slavery Society

Susan's passion and dedication for her cause soon gained attention in other circles. In 1856, she was approached by the American Anti-Slavery Society, an abolitionist group founded by William Lloyd Garrison, and asked to become its agent in New York state. Surprised and honored by the offer, Susan accepted it right away. One of her new responsibilities was arranging speaking tours to help spread the word against slavery in America. Susan, of course, intended to speak herself. She was not about to abandon her efforts in the women's rights movement. She would pursue two great causes at the same time. For the first time in her life, Susan was also paid for her social-reform work.

Susan took on her new post with her typical abundance of energy and enthusiasm. Her capacity for work and her apparent inability to sit still for long amazed her colleagues in the American Anti-Slavery Society. Unfortunately, Susan could not call upon many of her female friends to assist in her new endeavor. Most of them, like Elizabeth Cady Stanton, were married with children and preoccupied with domestic life. Advocates of women's rights remained a relatively small circle and became closely associated with the abolitionist movement. They depended on abolitionist resources and funding. They published their articles in abolitionist newspapers.

White Lady, happy, proud and free,
Lend awhile thine ear to me ;
Let the Negro Mother's wail
Turn thy pale cheek still more pale.
Can the Negro Mother joy
Over this her captive boy,
Which in bondage and in tears,
For a life of wo she rears ?
Though she bears a Mother's name,
A Mother's rights she may not claim ;
For the white man's will can part,
Her darling from her bursting heart.

From the Genius of Universal Emancipation.
LETTERS ON SLAVERY.—No. III.

This poem appeared in the antislavery newspaper *The Liberator,* which was published by abolitionist William Lloyd Garrison. Garrison founded the American Anti-Slavery Society.

When Lucy Stone, a prominent abolitionist and organizer in the women's rights movement, announced her plans to marry, Susan felt betrayed by her friend's decision. She lectured Stone on the need to stay focused on their larger goal and higher purpose. Eventually, Susan's friendship with Stone turned bitter. It was a repeat of what happened when Susan's sisters Guelma and Hannah had gotten married. Susan remained firmly convinced that marriage was an obstacle preventing women from gaining full equality in American society. Her falling-out with Stone would have negative repercussions down the road for the women's rights movement.

Meanwhile, Susan continued her speaking tour for the American Anti-Slavery Society, traveling across New York state. Many times, pro-slavery agents attempted to disrupt the meetings she organized, but Susan never gave in to their intimidation. However, her opposition grew in intensity as the division in the country deepened over the issue of slavery. On the eve of the Civil War, unruly mobs prevented Susan from speaking in every town on the circuit between Buffalo and Albany. In Rochester, the police had to escort Susan from the speakers' hall for her own safety.

Susan was a visionary, compared to her contemporaries, when it came to the issue of race. Most abolitionists were debating what should become of the slaves once they were set free. Susan, however, called for a fully integrated society where blacks and whites would be treated as equals. At the time, this was considered dangerously radical. Even people like Abraham Lincoln did not support this view. Lincoln himself proposed that the slaves should be sent to newly established colonies in Africa. Susan, however, insisted on full citizenship for African Americans.

Controversy and Disagreements

In 1860, Susan once again joined forces with Elizabeth Cady Stanton. The two women had fought hard over the last four years for an expanded version of the Married Women's Property Act. The expanded act was finally coming up for a vote. Susan arranged for Stanton to deliver three major speeches in three months' time. (The year before, Stanton gave birth to her seventh and last child.) In March, Stanton addressed the New York Judiciary Committee in Albany. Convinced by Stanton's passionate appeal, the state legislature passed the expanded act the day after her speech. Women in the state of New York now had the right to own property independently of their husbands, to keep all the money they earned, to sue (and be sued) in a court of law, and to share custody of their children. Together, Susan and Stanton had won the first great victory for the women's rights movement. They wasted no time in taking their battle into more controversial areas.

In May of that year, Susan arranged for Stanton to speak at Cooper Union in New York City for the 10th anniversary of the National Women's Rights Convention. Stanton's address focused on the institution of marriage, calling it "nothing more than legalized

Abolitionist and women's rights activist Lucy Stone (above) helped organize the women's rights movement in the United States. She was one of the first American women to lecture on women's rights.

prostitution." Only a "contract made by equal parties," she went on to say, would lead to a life of equality for both men and women. In her concluding remarks, Stanton suggested that marriage become a purely legal institution that either party should be able to end. Susan supported everything Stanton had to say, but most of the people in attendance were left stunned.

Lucy Stone had attempted to keep the whole issue of marriage off the agenda. While she agreed with Susan and Stanton that these things were essential for women to make any progress in society, she told them it should not be labeled as a women's rights issue as it "concerns men just as much." Antoinette Brown Blackwell, another friend of Susan's and the first woman to be ordained as a Protestant minister in the United States, insisted that marriage was permanent, ordained (ordered) by God, and cannot be undone. According to Blackwell, divorce was therefore "naturally and morally impossible." Wendell Phillips, the famous abolitionist and orator, not only opposed Stanton but also called for her inflammatory remarks to be stricken from the record. While the delegates at the convention allowed Stanton's words to remain on the record, they adjourned without voting on her resolution. Stanton's opponents in the press quickly seized upon her radical ideas and used the event to further defame the women's rights movement.

In December 1860, Susan and Stanton's relationship with many of their allies in the abolition movement deteriorated even further. It started when a woman named Phoebe Harris Phelps came to Susan asking for her help. She was in hiding from her husband, a Massachusetts Republican state senator. After suffering years of physical and mental abuse, Phoebe Phelps threatened to expose her husband's marital infidelities, but then things got worse. He took away her property, sent her to an insane asylum, and told her she would never see their children again. Not knowing what else to do, Phelps took her 13-year-old daughter and fled to New York. Susan found a place for them to stay and then informed her colleagues what she had done. When William Lloyd Garrison and Wendell Phillips learned of this, they demanded to know where Susan was hiding the woman and her child. Susan, however, refused to tell them. Garrison pointed out that Massachusetts state law gave husbands full guardianship over their children. Susan was appalled. She claimed that any law that gave fathers "ownership" over their children was wicked. She also reminded Garrison that he had helped many slaves escape to Canada in violation of an unjust law. The same law required that fugitive slaves be returned to their masters. Just as Garrison would never obey such an unjust law, Susan said she would rather die than give the child back to her father.

Susan never gave up Phelps and her daughter, but they were eventually returned to Massachusetts, where the father was given full custody of his child. This was too much for Susan to bear. She was now convinced that the men with whom she was battling the evil of slavery did not fully share her convictions about women's equality. In a letter to Lucy Stone, Susan complained that their male colleagues in the abolitionist movement wanted to postpone the issue of women's rights. "So let us do our own work," Susan wrote, "and in our own way." That work was delayed, however, when the country was engulfed in civil war.

Effects of the Civil War

In early 1861, Susan made all the arrangements for the annual National Women's Rights Convention. However, those plans were interrupted when the American Civil War broke out in April. People in the North were determined to prevent the rebellious South from seceding from the Union. With the outbreak of war, nothing else seemed to matter. The American Anti-Slavery Society canceled its convention that year. Most of Susan's colleagues in the women's rights movement, including Elizabeth Cady Stanton, urged her to do the same with the National Women's Rights Convention as a demonstration of support for the Union cause. Stanton and the others believed that if they backed the Union, the Republicans, the "Party of Lincoln," might show their gratitude by promoting woman suffrage once the war was over. Susan, however, was shocked and disturbed by this idea.

Raised as a Quaker, Susan was a lifelong pacifist and remained distrustful of the men who were taking the country to war. (A pacifist is an opponent of war.)

Susan considered Abraham Lincoln to be a "weak and trembling" politician from the prairie. The women's rights movement, she believed, could not afford to stop its struggle for equality, even for the war. When her colleagues urged her to suspend activities until the "war excitement" had died down, Susan accused them of acting like politicians. To cooperate with the U.S. government, which allowed the evil of slavery to

Susan helped the abolitionist Harriet Tubman (left) assist fugitive slaves on their way to Canada. Susan believed that the end of slavery was "the only possible compensation for this merciless" Civil War.

exist, she said, would be to act out of convenience, not principle. Susan did not think supporting the war would in any way help to achieve women's rights. She feared just the opposite would happen. She believed that the few gains they had made could be swept away during the war. Unfortunately, she was proven correct. In 1862, the New York state legislature revoked the provision of the Married Women's Act that gave mothers equal custody over their children. Disheartened, Susan retreated to the Anthony family's farm.

Susan's self-imposed isolation proved to be difficult for her. She busied herself with whatever she could find to do. Once again, she took part in the farm's daily chores. She washed every window in the house and supervised the plowing in the fields. When this was not enough, she joined a sewing club but found the women in it to have little intelligence. She attended meetings of the Society of Friends but thought they were too "namby-pamby" (weak). She went to an African American church to hear Frederick Douglass speak and assisted fugitive slaves on their way to Canada with the help of the abolitionist Harriet Tubman. Still, Susan wanted to do more. She grew increasingly frustrated with how the Union was conducting the war. She hoped the government would move quickly to free every slave. In Susan's mind, the end of slavery was "the only possible compensation for this merciless war." All the while, she never stopped thinking about what she could do to advance the cause of women's rights.

CHAPTER 3

Women's Rights in America

The Women's National Loyal League

In January 1863, Susan's chance to do more came in the form of a letter from Elizabeth Cady Stanton's husband, Henry. Two years earlier, the Stantons had moved from Seneca Falls to New York City so that Henry could assume his new post as deputy collector of the port of New York City. On New Year's Day, Lincoln's Emancipation Proclamation had gone into effect. It freed enslaved people in the rebellious states of the Confederacy but said nothing about those living inside the Union. Charles Sumner, a Republican senator from Massachusetts, was proposing an amendment to the United States Constitution to abolish slavery in America, but it was not clear if it would have enough support in the U.S. Congress to send it on to the states for ratification. Writing to Susan, Henry Stanton suggested that women in the North could make all the difference if they rallied behind this cause. Susan jumped at the opportunity.

By February, Susan was living in the Stantons' home in New York City and thinking of ways to organize and inspire the women in the North. On May 14, she and Elizabeth Cady Stanton, with the help of Lucy Stone and others, established the Women's National Loyal League. It was the first nationwide women's political organization in the United States. It was a turning point in the history of the women's rights movement. It went from a loosely structured undertaking to a highly organized association. The league was founded with the express purpose of campaigning for an amendment to the Constitution that would abolish slavery in America once and for all. The organization amassed a membership of about 5,000. Stanton once again served as president of the organization, with Susan serving as secretary. She was also responsible for recruiting and organizing some 2,000 volunteers across the country.

Susan and her volunteers began to "canvass the nation for freedom." They obtained almost 400,000 signatures for the abolition of slavery, in the largest petition drive up to that point in the nation's history. The collection of names represented approximately one out of every 24 adults in the Northern States. On February 9, 1864, Charles Sumner presented the signed petitions to the U.S. Senate.

By the summer of 1864, when it became clear that the Thirteenth Amendment was going to pass, the Women's National Loyal League disbanded. It had attained its lofty goal and so much more. In combining the fight to end slavery with the struggle to achieve women's rights, the league demonstrated the power of political action at a "grassroots" level at a time when only men had the right to vote in the United States. It also laid the groundwork for a new generation of women activists. Among them was Anna Elizabeth Dickinson. A gifted speaker at a young age, Dickinson was the first woman to give a political address to the U.S. Congress. There was now a broad network of female activists whom Susan could call upon to revive the women's rights movement. The Thirteenth Amendment to the Constitution, which ended slavery in the United States, was ratified on December 6, 1865. Afterward, Senator Sumner praised the "noble work" of the women of the North who had helped to make it possible.

Susan had great hopes for the future. For well over a decade, she had worked with abolitionists to end slavery in America. Time and again, she had deferred to the men who led the movement in the hope of gaining equality for all people—blacks and whites, men and women. Now, in early 1865, with the end of the Civil War approaching, the end to the terrible injustice of slavery was in sight. To Susan and her allies, giving the formerly enslaved people the right to vote seemed the next logical step. After that, they hoped—and expected—the women of America would be given the same right, which they had been fighting for since 1848.

Susan spent the better part of 1865 with her brother, Daniel, in Kansas. Daniel, who would go on to be the mayor of Leavenworth, Kansas, had become something of a social activist himself. He and Susan's other brother, Jacob Merritt, had taken part in the pre–Civil War border conflict known as "Bleeding Kansas." (Bleeding Kansas refers to a period of violence between proslavery and antislavery groups in Kansas and Missouri in the early 1860's. More than 50 people were killed in the violence.) The two Anthony men had fought alongside the famed abolitionist John Brown, whose career came to an end in 1859 when he raided the U.S. military arsenal at Harpers Ferry, Virginia, to steal weapons in support of a slave uprising. During her time with Daniel,

A PETITION

FOR

UNIVERSAL SUFFRAGE.

To the Senate and House of Representatives:

The undersigned, Women of the United States, respectfully ask an amendment of the Constitution that shall prohibit the several States from disfranchising any of their citizens on the ground of sex.

In making our demand for Suffrage, we would call your attention to the fact that we represent fifteen million people—one half the entire population of the country—intelligent, virtuous, native-born American citizens; and yet stand outside the pale of political recognition.

The Constitution classes us as "free people," and counts us *whole* persons in the basis of representation; and yet are we governed without our consent, compelled to pay taxes without appeal, and punished for violations of law without choice of judge or juror.

The experience of all ages, the Declarations of the Fathers, the Statute Laws of our own day, and the fearful revolution through which we have just passed, all prove the uncertain tenure of life, liberty and property so long as the ballot—the only weapon of self-protection—is not in the hand of every citizen.

Therefore, as you are now amending the Constitution, and, in harmony with advancing civilization, placing new safeguards round the individual rights of four millions of emancipated slaves, we ask that you extend the right of Suffrage to Woman—the only remaining class of disfranchised citizens—and thus fulfil your Constitutional obligation "to Guarantee to every State in the Union a Republican form of Government."

As all partial application of Republican principles must ever breed a complicated legislation as well as a discontented people, we would pray your Honorable Body, in order to simplify the machinery of government and ensure domestic tranquillity, that you legislate hereafter for persons, citizens, tax-payers, and not for class or caste.

For justice and equality your petitioners will ever pray.

NAMES.	RESIDENCE.
Elizabeth Cady Stanton	New York
Susan B. Anthony	Rochester — N.Y.
Antoinette Brown Blackwell	New York
Lucy Stone	Newark N. Jersey
Joanna S. Morse	48 Livingston. Brooklyn
Ernestine L. Rose	New York
Harriet E. Eaton	6, West 14th Street N.Y.
Catharine C. Wilkeson	83 Clinton Place New York
Elizabeth R. Tilton	48 Livingston St. Brooklyn
Mary Fowler Gilbert	293 W. 19" St New York
Mary E. Gilbert	New York
M. Griffith	New York.

Susan, along with women's rights leaders Elizabeth Cady Stanton, Lucy Stone, and others, signed this petition for a constitutional amendment for universal suffrage.

Susan helped him develop his abolitionist newspaper. When she received a letter from Elizabeth Cady Stanton that a new amendment to the Constitution (one proposing citizenship for African Americans) required her help, Susan decided to head back East.

The American Equal Rights Association

When she arrived in New York, Susan realized a long, hard road lay ahead. In May, the American Anti-Slavery Society had met to decide on its future. Its leader, William Lloyd Garrison, thought the struggle to end slavery was over. With the liberation of the enslaved people in the United States, he felt his job was done and called for his organization to be disbanded. Wendell Phillips, however, believed the society still had work to do. The institution of slavery had ended, but a good deal of injustice remained to be dealt with.

Susan (seated) with the famous abolitionist Wendell Phillips and an unidentified woman. Susan and Phillips were allies in the struggle for equal rights.

He felt that the freedom of the people who had been enslaved would never be guaranteed unless they had the right to vote. While Susan and Phillips had their share of disagreements over the years, the two remained allies. They worked along with Stanton and others toward gaining suffrage for the millions of African Americans living in the former Confederacy.

When Phillips won the presidency of a revitalized Anti-Slavery Society, he gave an inaugural address to a large assembly. He told his listeners that the struggle ahead of them would not be an easy one. Millions of men in the Democratic and Republican parties would have to be won over. However, Phillips believed that convincing these men

that the time had come to grant women the right to
vote as well was simply too much to ask. He declared
that the issue of woman suffrage would therefore have
to wait. Recalling Abraham Lincoln's words, he said
they should fight one war at a time. "This," he added,
"is the Negro's hour."

Susan considered Phillips' speech as a betrayal.
She felt it violated the basic principles of what she was
fighting for. In her mind, the struggle of the last 20
years was about equality—of blacks and whites, of men
and women. As such, all people of the United States
had a basic right to full citizenship. To allow one group
to vote at the expense of another contradicted everything that the women's rights movement had been
hoping to achieve since 1848. Susan remained firm in
her belief that all men and women must be given the
right to vote. She felt that if the focus remained on full
citizenship for African American men, the cause of
women might be held back for at least a generation.

After Wendell Phillips' speech, Susan and Stanton
wasted no time in organizing a drive to collect 10,000
signatures to petition the U.S. Congress to include
woman suffrage in the proposed Fourteenth Amendment. Charles Sumner called their efforts a "most
inopportune" endeavor, and the so-called "Radical
Republicans" refused to submit the petition to Congress. Frustrated, Susan and Stanton began to feel that
their own colleagues were placing obstacles in their
way. Not only did the new amendment fail to mention
woman suffrage, it referred to voters as "male citizens."
For the first time in its long history, the Constitution
was to include a gender-specific distinction. Susan said

she would rather cut off her right hand "than ask the ballot for the black man and not the woman." The proposed amendment was also unpopular among many abolitionists, as it did not guarantee African American men the right to vote. It simply provided them equal protection under the law.

In the face of this setback, Susan and Stanton turned their attention to reviving the women's rights movement. On May 10, 1866, they held the 11th National Woman's Rights Convention, the first one held since the Civil War began. During the meeting, Susan proposed a resolution calling for the women's movement to join forces with the Anti-Slavery Society and become the American Equal Rights Association (AERA). Susan's proposal was adopted unanimously by the convention. The new organization's purpose would be to gain equal rights for all American citizens, most especially the right to vote. The leadership of the AERA included many prominent men and women. Among them were Frederick Douglass, Lucretia Mott, and Lucy Stone. However, the AERA's goal of universal suffrage was resisted by other leaders in the abolitionist movement and their allies in the Republican Party. They maintained that campaigning for woman suffrage would only hinder their efforts to win the vote for African American men.

In June 1866, Congress passed the Fourteenth Amendment and sent it to the states to be ratified.

Full citizenship for African Americans was now within reach. That summer, a wave of violence swept across the South as white mobs viciously attacked African Americans. Because of this, the Radical Republicans began to doubt if black suffrage could be achieved anytime soon. They realized that further amendments to the Constitution would likely be needed to ensure that African Americans would not face discrimination at the polls. When Susan and the other leaders of the AERA heard this, they feared that the issue of woman suffrage would face yet another delay. They knew they would need to build up support to attain their goal.

In 1867, the AERA was given two fronts on which to battle for women's rights. Kansas had two major referenda on the state ballot that year. For the first time in the United States, those eligible to vote were to weigh in on the issue of suffrage for both African Americans and women. At the same time, the state of New York held a constitutional convention. Lucy Stone and her husband rushed to Kansas to run the AERA's campaign there. Meanwhile, Susan launched a new petition drive in New York with the help of Elizabeth Cady Stanton. Susan and Stanton once again visited all the counties in the state, gathering the signatures of more than 28,000 women petitioning for the right to vote. Unfortunately, their efforts were in vain. Horace Greeley, the founder and editor of the influential *New-York Tribune* newspaper, chose not to support the AERA, even though he had been an early advocate of women's rights. Greeley thought that black suffrage should take precedence over woman suffrage.

He claimed that the public "does not demand, and would not sustain, an innovation so revolutionary and sweeping" as giving women the right to vote. The *New-York Tribune* would remain opposed to the AERA until Greeley's death in 1872. Susan and Stanton were infuriated by his withholding of support.

The AERA's campaign in Kansas fared little better. When Susan and Stanton arrived there in September, the situation looked grim. The Republican Party refused to endorse woman suffrage, and some of its leaders were actively campaigning against it. Most abolitionist newspapers ignored the issue, focusing instead on the need to win the vote for African American men. Like Horace Greeley, Wendell Phillips opposed mixing the two causes of black suffrage and woman suffrage. In charge of financing the campaign for woman suffrage, Phillips refused to let any of the money be used in Kansas. Susan and Stanton felt betrayed by the so-called "liberal" men who had until now been their allies. The two women were dejected, without funds, and facing defeat at the polls. Unwilling to give up the fight, however, Susan and Stanton went on the road, crisscrossing the state to drum up support.

They unleashed a storm of controversy when they accepted help from George Francis Train. An eccentric millionaire, Train was a freethinking Democrat who advocated women's rights but did not support black suffrage due to his racist views. Susan and Train campaigned together in the final weeks before the election. Susan would speak first and then allow Train to deliver his remarks. Unfortunately, Train unleashed the worst kind of bigotry against African Americans in his speeches, belittling their intelligence and claiming they were dishonest by nature. Whatever she may have thought of Train's views, Susan never protested publicly against them. Train's financial backing and his commitment to women's rights were enough to earn her silence. She had spent the last 20 years fighting for the rights of African Americans, but Susan was desperate to win the right to vote for women. All other considerations paled in comparison to this all-important issue. Later, Susan told a friend that Train was the only man she ever met who could "move mountains." In the end, however, Train's support did not make any difference to the voters in Kansas. Just as in New York, woman suffrage, as well as suffrage for African Americans, went down in defeat.

Susan set off a storm of controversy by accepting financial backing from millionaire George Francis Train (above), who did not support black suffrage because of his racist views.

The Revolution

The struggle to gain women the right to vote would continue for the next 50 years. Susan and her colleagues kept up a near-constant pressure. They organized campaign after campaign aimed at giving the men of America the opportunity to vote for woman

The Revolution.

PRINCIPLE, NOT POLICY: JUSTICE, NOT FAVORS.

VOL. I.—NO. 1.　　　NEW YORK, WEDNESDAY, JANUARY 8, 1868.　　　$2.00 A YEAR.

The Revolution;

THE ORGAN OF THE

NATIONAL PARTY OF NEW AMERICA.

PRINCIPLE, NOT POLICY—INDIVIDUAL RIGHTS AND RESPONSIBILITIES.

THE REVOLUTION WILL ADVOCATE:

1. IN POLITICS—Educated Suffrage, Irrespective of Sex or Color; Equal Pay to Women for Equal Work; Eight Hours Labor; Abolition of Standing Armies and Party Despotisms. Down with Politicians—Up with the People!

2. IN RELIGION—Deeper Thought; Broader Idea; Science not Superstition; Personal Purity; Love to Man as well as God.

3. IN SOCIAL LIFE.—Morality and Reform; Practical Education, not Theoretical; Facts not Fiction; Virtue not Vice; Cold Water not Alcoholic Drinks or Medicines. It will indulge in no Gross Personalities and insert no Quack or Immoral Advertisements, so common even in Religious Newspapers.

4. THE REVOLUTION proposes a new Commercial and Financial Policy. America no longer led by Europe. Gold like our Cotton and Corn for sale. Greenbacks for money. An American System of Finance. American Products and Labor Free. Foreign Manufactures Prohibited. Open doors to Artisans and Immigrants. Atlantic and Pacific Oceans for American Steamships and Shipping; or American goods in American bottoms. New York the Financial Centre of the World. Wall Street emancipated from Bank of England, or American Cash for American Bills. The Credit Foncier and Credit Mobilier System, or Capital Mobilized to Resuscitate the South and our Mining Interests, and to People the Country from Ocean to Ocean, from Omaha to San Francisco. More organized Labor, more Cotton, more Gold and Silver Bullion to sell foreigners at the highest prices. Ten millions of Naturalized Citizens DEMAND A PENNY OCEAN POSTAGE, to Strengthen the Brotherhood of Labor; and if Congress Vote One Hundred and Twenty-five Millions for a Standing Army and Freedman's Bureau, cannot they spare One Million to Educate Europe and to keep bright the chain of acquaintance and friendship between those millions and their fatherland?

Send in your Subscription. THE REVOLUTION, published weekly, will be the Great Organ of the Age.

TERMS.—Two dollars a year, in advance. Ten names ($20) entitle the sender to one copy free.

ELIZABETH CADY STANTON, } EDS.
PARKER PILLSBURY, }

SUSAN B. ANTHONY,
Proprietor and Manager.
37 Park Row (Room 17), New York City,
To whom address all business letters.

KANSAS.

THE question of the enfranchisement of woman has already passed the court of moral discussion, and is now fairly ushered into the arena of politics, where it must remain a fixed element of debate, until party necessity shall compel its success.

With 9,000 votes in Kansas, one-third the entire vote, every politician must see that the friends of "woman's suffrage" hold the balance of power in that State to-day. And those 9,000 votes represent a principle deep in the hearts of the people, for this triumph was secured without money, without a press, without a party. With these instrumentalities now fast coming to us on all sides, the victory in Kansas is but the herald of greater victories in every State of the Union. Kansas already leads the world in her legislation for woman on questions of property, education, wages, marriage and divorce. Her best universities are open alike to boys and girls. In fact woman has a voice in the legislation of that State. She votes on all school questions and is eligible to the office of trustee. She has a voice in temperance too; no license is granted without the consent of a majority of the adult citizens, male and female, black and white. The consequence is, stone school houses are voted up in every part of the State, and rum voted down. Many of the ablest men in that State are champions of woman's cause. Governors, judges, lawyers and clergymen. Two-thirds of the press and pulpits advocate the idea, in spite of the opposition of politicians. The first Governor of Kansas, twice chosen to that office, Charles Robinson, went all through the State, speaking every day for two months in favor of woman's suffrage. In the organization of the State government, he proposed that the words "white female" should not be inserted in the Kansas constitution. All this shows that giving political rights to women is no new idea in that State. Who that has listened with tearful eyes to the deep experiences of those Kansas women, through the darkest hours of their history, does not feel that such bravery and self denial as they have shown alike in war and peace, have richly earned for them the crown of citizenship.

Opposed to this moral sentiment of the liberal minds of the State, many adverse influences were brought to bear through the entire campaign.

The action of the New York Constitutional Convention; the silence of eastern journals on the question; the opposition of abolitionists lest a demand for woman's suffrage should defeat negro suffrage; the hostility everywhere of black men themselves; some even stumping the State against woman's suffrage; the official action of both the leading parties in their conventions in Leavensworth against the proposition, with every organized Republican influence outside as well as inside the State, all combined might have made our vote comparatively a small one, had not George Francis Train gone into the State two weeks before the election and galvanized the Democrats into their duty, thus securing 9,000 votes for woman's suffrage. Some claim that we are indebted to the Republicans for this vote; but the fact that the most radical republican district, Douglass County, gave the largest vote against woman's suffrage, while Leavenworth, the Democratic district, gave the largest vote for it, fully settles that question.

In saying that Mr. Train helped to swell our vote takes nothing from the credit due all those who labored faithfully for months in that State. All praise to Olympia Brown, Lucy Stone, Susan B. Anthony, Henry B. Blackwell, and Judge Wood, who welcomed, for an idea, the hardships of travelling in a new State, fording streams, scaling rocky brinks, sleeping on the ground and eating hard tack, with the fatigue of constant speaking, in school-houses, barns, mills, depots and the open air; and especially, all praise to the glorious Hutchinson family—John, his son Henry and daughter, Viola—who, with their own horses and carriage, made the entire circuit of the state, singing Woman's Suffrage into souls that logic could never penetrate. Having shared with them the hardships, with them I rejoice in our success.

E. C. S.

THE BALLOT—BREAD, VIRTUE, POWER.

THE REVOLUTION will contain a series of articles, beginning next week, to prove the power of the ballot in elevating the character and condition of woman. We shall show that the ballot will secure for woman equal place and equal wages in the world of work; that it will open to her the schools, colleges, professions and all the opportunities and advantages of life; that in her hand it will be a moral power to stay the tide of vice and crime and misery on every side. In the words of Bishop Simpson—

"We believe that the great vices in our large cities will never be conquered until the ballot is put in the hands of women. If the question of the danger of their sons being drawn away into drinking saloons was brought up, if the mothers had the power, they would close them; if the sisters had the power, and they saw their brothers going away to haunts of infamy, they would close those places. You may get men to trifle with purity, with virtue, with righteousness; but, thank God, the hearts of the women of our land—the mothers, wives and daughters—are too pure to make a compromise either with intemperance or licentiousness."

Thus, too, shall we purge our constitutions and statute laws from all invidious distinctions among the citizens of the States, and secure the same civil and moral code for man and woman. We will show the hundred thousand female teachers, and the millions of laboring women, that their complaints, petitions, strikes and protective unions are of no avail until they hold the ballot in their own hands; for it is the first step toward social, religious and political equality.

suffrage. They were met with stiff resistance. Nevertheless, Susan believed that the tide was beginning to turn. Despite all the obstacles they faced in the 1867 election, woman suffrage had gained one-third of the overall vote. George Francis Train also came through on one of the promises he made during the campaign. He had promised financial help so that Susan and Stanton could start a newspaper of their own. Susan had spent years pleading with distrustful publishers and editors across the United States to give the women's rights movement fair coverage in their newspapers. Now, thanks to Train, the women's rights movement had its own weekly paper called *The Revolution*. Excited, Susan wrote to a friend that the 16-page newspaper would be an instrument "through which we can make our own claim in our own time."

Even so, some of Susan and Stanton's associates remained troubled by their political alliance with Train. They accused the two women of abandoning their principles. In private, Lucy Stone condemned Susan for "making a spectacle of herself." When Susan and Stanton returned to New York, the AERA's executive board requested a meeting. The board members wanted to know why the two women had placed ads in newspapers supporting Train. They also asked Susan and Stanton why they had used the names of other members of the AERA without their permission. During the meeting, Susan erupted in anger. According to Lucy Stone, she said, "I am the Equal Rights Association. Not one of you amounts to shucks except for me!" When William Lloyd Garrison raised his concerns that Train was stirring up

In 1868, the women's rights movement published its own weekly newspaper, *The Revolution* (left).

racial fears in the country, Susan still would not back down. She contradicted her accusers by saying it was all a simple matter of jealousy: She had a newspaper and they did not. Little by little, Susan and Stanton's relationship with many of their associates continued to break down.

On January 8, 1868, the first issue of *The Revolution* appeared. Focusing primarily on women's rights, especially the importance of winning the vote, it also covered the labor movement, finance, and politics in general. Closely following the end of the Civil War, the practice of slavery had been outlawed in the United States. After this great victory, many of the abolitionist newspapers that had promoted social reform went out of business. Susan hoped *The Revolution* would fill this void, while providing a forum for an exchange of ideas on the issues that affected women across the country. Its slogan was "Principle, not policy; justice, not favors—men, their rights and nothing more; women, their rights and nothing less."

Stanton served as co-editor of the newspaper with a man named Parker Pillsbury, a Congregational minister, longtime abolitionist, and supporter of women's rights from New England. Once again, Susan did much of the organizational work. Week after week, *The Revolution* attacked the Republican Party for its lack of loyalty to the cause of women's rights. It also supported labor unions' right to strike and called for

> *"Principle, not policy; justice, not favors—men, their rights and nothing more; women, their rights and nothing less."*

equal pay for equal work. With its aggressive style, the paper also widened the gulf between Susan and Stanton and many of their old allies in the women's rights movement. Lucy Stone found *The Revolution* to be a complete embarrassment. She warned that it would anger their Republican base and detract from their efforts to gain women the right to vote.

An Alliance with Labor

In 1866, several labor unions across the United States came together to form the National Labor Union (NLU). The NLU reached out to farmers, African Americans, and women in the hope of creating a broad-based political organization. *The Revolution* responded with great enthusiasm, declaring that the principles of the NLU are "our principles." It boldly predicted that the alliance between working-class men, women, and African Americans would "speedily wrest the sceptre from … the land monopolists, the bond-holders, the politicians." Both Susan and Stanton were named as delegates to the NLU Congress in 1868.

Unfortunately, the alliance with the NLU did not last long. The following year, after a printers' strike broke out, Susan supported a training program sponsored by the company owners that provided women with a set of skills that would allow them to replace the men who were on strike. Susan saw this as an opportunity for women to branch out in a trade from which women were often excluded. This did not go over well with the leadership of the NLU. At its 1869 Congress, Susan was once again named as a delegate. However, due to overwhelming opposition, she was almost immediately removed from office. Many accused her of weakening the unions because of her lack of support during the printers' strike.

Susan also worked with the newly formed Working Women's Association (WWA) to try to establish labor unions for women only. However, this met with little success. Nevertheless, the WWA did not limit itself to only assisting women in the trades. The organization had a commitment to a broader base of "wrongs against women." It was for this reason that Susan and the WWA took on the case of Hester Vaughan. Vaughan was a young immigrant from Gloucestershire, England, who came to America to be with her new husband. However, he turned out to be already married and Vaughan soon found herself alone. She found work in Philadelphia as a domestic servant for various families but struggled to make ends meet. Before long, she became pregnant. During a bout of illness after giving birth, she failed to take care of her baby and it died. Vaughan was charged with infanticide, the killing of an infant. She was sentenced to death and taken to prison. Claiming that society and the law treated women unfairly, the WWA organized a rally where Susan spoke in defense of Vaughan. The WWA also sent some of its members to visit Vaughan in prison and petitioned the governor of Pennsylvania to pardon her, which he eventually did. With Stanton's help, Susan raised enough money to return Vaughan to England. Susan's work with the WWA on the Vaughan case was an example of how she used her nationwide reputation and influence to help less fortunate women.

Division and Transformation

While Susan tried to make new allies among the labor unions, old friends were falling by the wayside. In November 1868, Lucy Stone helped to found a new organization called the New England Woman Suffrage Association (NEWSA). Its first president was Julia Ward Howe, a poet and author best known for writing "The Battle Hymn of the Republic." Among NEWSA's members were Antoinette Brown Blackwell, Abigail Kelley Foster, Frederick Douglass, and many other influential suffragists based in the Boston, Massachusetts, area. Lucy Stone had never gotten over Susan and Stanton's work with George Francis Train, and their opposition to the proposed Fifteenth Amendment to the U.S. Constitution made matters worse.

The new amendment was intended to further protect the rights of formerly enslaved people. It prohibited the state and federal governments from

Lucy Stone helped to found the New England Woman Suffrage Association in 1868. Its first president was poet and author Julia Ward Howe, best known for writing "The Battle Hymn of the Republic."

denying any citizen the right to vote based on "race, color, or previous condition of servitude." This was the third and last of the "Reconstruction Amendments" proposed by the Radical Republicans to give equal rights and protection to African Americans. The reason Susan and Stanton opposed the Fifteenth Amendment was that the Republican Party once again expected that the issue of woman suffrage should wait. Lucy Stone and many other members of NEWSA regretted that the right to vote for both African Americans and women could not be pushed through together, but they thought the Fifteenth Amendment was a giant step in the right direction for the rights of all people. Susan's patience, however, was running out. She feared the U.S. Congress would be less willing to alter the Constitution in favor of women's rights after three amendments in the span of just five years.

In February 1869, Congress passed the Fifteenth Amendment and sent it to the states for ratification. Susan and Stanton wasted no time in heading to the Midwest to rally opposition against it. At the same time, they proposed another amendment to the Constitution that would finally give women the right to vote. Susan and Stanton received an enthusiastic welcome in every state they visited. Women throughout the country enthusiastically backed Susan and Stanton's proposal for universal suffrage. Most of their supporters, however, refused to oppose the Fifteenth Amendment. Unlike Susan, most women in the country seemed content to wait their turn. Susan and Stanton realized their campaign against the Fifteenth

Amendment was not working. They decided to change tactics.

In May, the annual convention of the AERA took place at Steinway Hall in New York City. Lucy Stone and the other leaders of NEWSA attended in the hope of resolving their differences with Susan and Stanton. The leaders of NEWSA shared in their desire for an amendment to the Constitution that would guarantee women the right to vote. Stone and the others also felt they needed Susan and Stanton's supporters to achieve their mutual goal. Settling their differences did not seem likely, however, as there was so much bad blood

Susan and Elizabeth Cady Stanton refused to support the Fifteenth Amendment (illustrated below) because they felt the issue of woman suffrage should not have to wait any longer.

between the factions. When the abolitionist Stephen Foster rose to speak, he asked Susan and Stanton to withdraw their membership from the AERA. Foster's words were difficult for Susan to hear. She had known him longer than her close friend and ally, Elizabeth Cady Stanton. Foster accused the two women of publicly rejecting the principles of the AERA by refusing to reject the racism of George Francis Train and attempting to defeat the Fifteenth Amendment. He also implied that Susan had not been honest about the AERA's money she spent during the campaign in Kansas. Susan was outraged and shouted back, "That is false!"

Henry Blackwell, Lucy Stone's husband, stepped in and did his best to ease the situation. Blackwell pointed out that Train was no longer an associate of Susan or Stanton, and he asked that everyone put that disagreeable episode behind them. (Shortly after the first issue of *The Revolution* came out, Train had sailed for England and ended up in prison for supporting Irish independence.) Blackwell went on to say that no one could doubt either Susan or Stanton's commitment to achieving equal rights. He added that the executive board was satisfied with Susan's financial records. After Blackwell's remarks, Stanton asked for a vote of confidence from the board and received it.

Frederick Douglass then asked to speak. He told the two women that he admired them greatly and considered them to be friends, but some of their views on African Americans as reported in *The Revolution* had hurt him deeply. He was determined to find common ground. In response, Susan offered two resolutions for the leadership of the AERA to consider. The first proposed opposition to the Fifteenth Amendment; the second called for "educated suffrage" to be added to the organization's platform. If they could not give "the whole loaf of justice" to the American people, at least give it to the most capable and intelligent. "It is intelligence … [and] morality that is needed now," she urged. This only caused the debate to intensify. In the end, Susan and Stanton went down in defeat. The convention voted against educated suffrage and overwhelmingly supported the Fifteenth Amendment. After this explosive encounter, the AERA effectively disbanded.

Discouraged and further alienated from their old allies, Susan and Stanton were determined to move ahead with their agenda. Two days after the final meeting of the AERA, they formed a new organization called the National Woman Suffrage Association (NWSA). Hoping to achieve great things, the NWSA had a broad platform. It opposed approval of the Fifteenth Amendment, campaigned for another amendment that would grant women the right to vote, and advocated reform of the divorce laws, equal pay for women, and an eight-hour workday. Once again, Stanton became president and men were not allowed to hold office in the NWSA.

In response, Lucy Stone and the other leaders of the Boston-based NEWSA met in Cleveland, Ohio, in November 1869 and formed an organization of their own called the American Woman Suffrage Association (AWSA). Stone claimed the country needed a national organization that supported woman suffrage but that did not oppose the Fifteenth Amendment and lacked the negative tone of *The Revolution*. The AWSA, in Stone's words, would not use the methods which Stanton and Susan used.

Susan made an appearance at the AWSA's inaugural (first) meeting and gave a half-hearted promise to cooperate. Stone, however, was convinced that cooperation with Susan and Stanton was no longer possible. When she and Julia Ward Howe launched the AWSA's weekly suffragist publication called the *Woman's Journal,* they did so on the second anniversary of *The Revolution's* premiere to spite their former associates. This rivalry created an atmosphere of hostility that would last for decades and negatively affect the cause of women's rights. Ironically, the Fifteenth Amendment, the immediate cause for the split, was ratified by the states in February 1870 and was no longer a source of disagreement. Despite this division, the struggle to achieve woman suffrage did not slow down. In fact, it was about to accelerate, and Susan would come to stand center stage in the national debate.

CHAPTER 4

The National Suffrage Movement

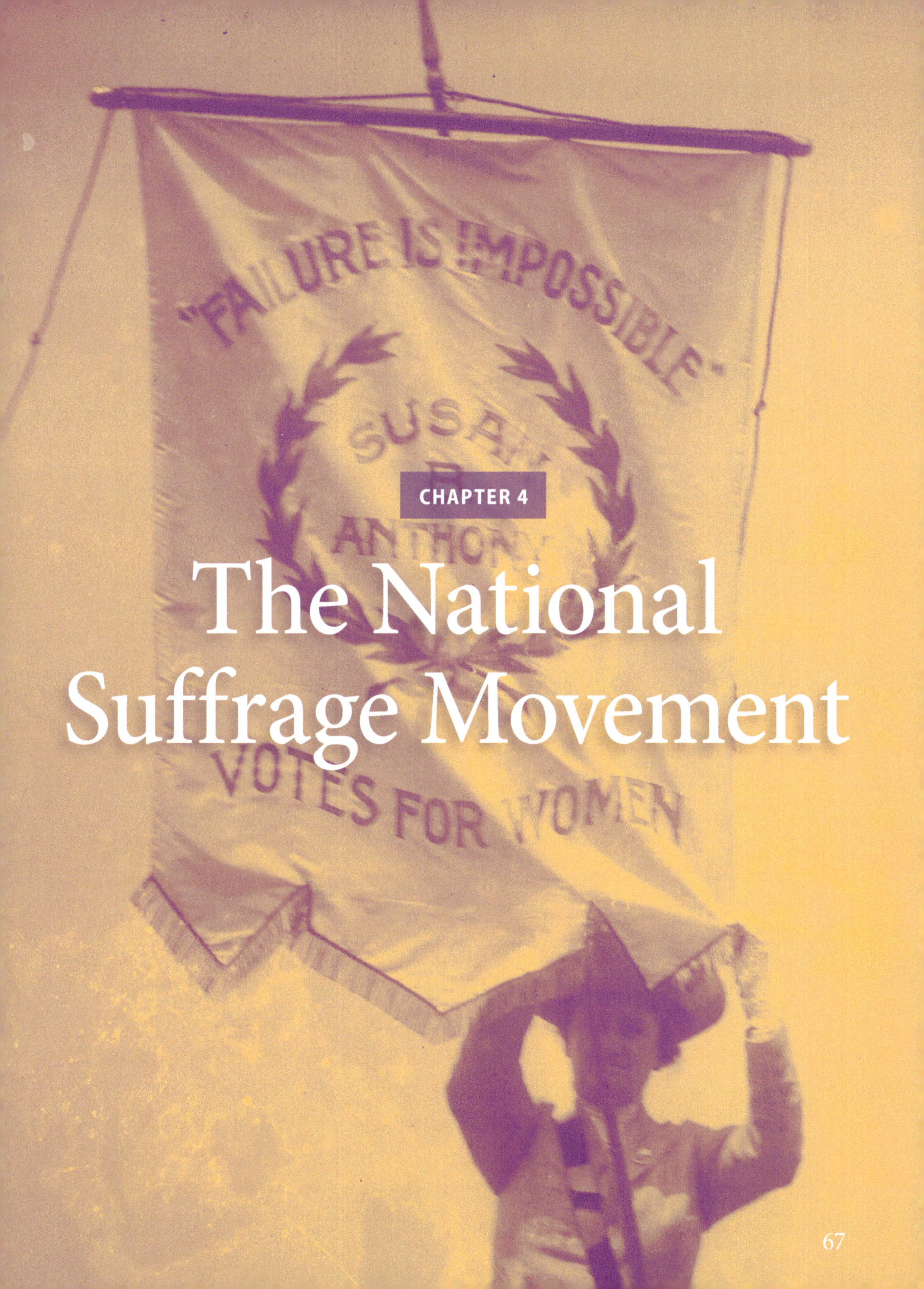

Taking the National Stage

By 1870, Susan had emerged as a nationally recognized leader in the struggle to achieve equal rights. She did so at a time when a single woman in her 50's was often regarded with disapproval and outright suspicion. The fact that Susan remained unmarried did not get in her way. In fact, because of the laws that regulated the ability of women to work, she used it to her advantage. For one thing, her profitable career on the lecture circuit would not have been possible if she had been married. At the time, married women were not allowed to sign contracts since their husbands usually took care of all financial matters.

As it turned out, the money that Susan made giving speeches came in handy. Almost immediately after its debut, *The Revolution* ran into financial problems. It had never had more than 3,000 subscribers, and the *Woman's Journal* gave it stiff competition. Susan tried desperately to keep *The Revolution* afloat. She raised subscription rates, exhausted her own savings, and borrowed money from family and friends. Harriet Beecher Stowe, who wrote the anti-slavery novel *Uncle Tom's Cabin*, offered to help if the paper's name and harsh tone could be changed, but Susan declined. Facing mounting debts, she and Stanton were forced to sell their newspaper after just 29 months of publication. Susan was deeply disappointed, even though selling the paper was necessary. She said it felt like "signing my own death warrant." The new owner was Laura Curtis Bullard, a wealthy writer and women's rights activist who gave *The Revolution* a more moderate tone. The selling price was $1. Susan personally assumed the paper's $10,000 debt, which she paid off through her work on the lecture circuit over the next six years.

When the press heard that *The Revolution* had been sold, there were widespread theories that Susan and Stanton had had a falling-out. Unfortunately, there was some truth behind the assumptions. Stanton remained devoted to the cause of woman suffrage, but she was beginning to grow tired of the intrigue and backbiting in the politics of the women's rights movement. Stanton only attended meetings of the NWSA occasionally, and this annoyed Susan. Another reason that kept Stanton from participating to Susan's liking was Stanton's lack of funds. When Stanton did not attend the NWSA convention in January 1871, Susan scolded her by saying, "How you can excuse yourself is more than I can understand." Things began to improve, however, when Stanton joined her on the lecture circuit and began making a little money.

In June of that year, the two women went on a speaking tour together, traveling from Chicago, Illinois, to San Francisco, California. Their timing seemed right, since the country was beginning to take seriously the debate over woman suffrage. They were also able to recruit new members to their cause. Because of this, the women's rights movement grew at the local and state levels and developed a strong, nationwide organization. Together, Susan and Stanton planned national conventions, lobbied Congress, and took their message to every corner of the country. Before long, however, Stanton was forced to return home to take care of her ailing mother. Susan pressed on without her, making her way to Oregon and Washington. She often endured difficult travel conditions and "horrid" food. As she went from town to town, the press was often scornful and even hostile toward Susan. These attacks often depressed her, but she did her best to take them in stride.

The United States vs. Susan B. Anthony

In the 1872 presidential election, Susan decided to up the stakes in the national debate on woman suffrage. She was inspired by an incident that took place three years earlier. A St. Louis, Missouri, lawyer named Francis Minor and his wife, Virginia, claimed that women already had the right to vote based on the wording of the recently adopted Fourteenth Amendment. It said, in part, that, "All persons born or naturalized in the United States … are citizens of the United States and of the State wherein they reside. No State shall make or enforce any law which shall abridge the privileges or immunities of citizens of the United States." Following this logic, the Minors argued that women, as citizens of the country, were eligible to vote at the polls. Susan thought it was a skillful action. She and Stanton urged women all over the country to exercise their rights and attempt to vote. Susan intended to lead the way herself.

On November 1, 1872, Susan and her three sisters showed up at their polling place in Rochester, New York, and demanded to be registered to vote. When the three male electoral registrars politely refused, Susan did not give in. She promised to pay the young men's fines if the government prosecuted them. Two of the three gave in, adding Susan, her sisters, and 10 other women to the voter rolls of Rochester's Eighth Ward. Susan could barely contain her excitement. On Election Day, she and six other women returned and cast their ballot to re-elect President Ulysses S. Grant and the Republican Party. Immediately afterward, Susan exclaimed to Stanton that she had "gone and done it!"

Naturally, Susan's bold exploit was headline news in Rochester and across the country. For the three weeks that followed, nothing happened. Then, on Thanksgiving Day, a U.S. marshal arrived on the doorstep of Susan's home with a warrant for her arrest. The man was extremely polite and told Susan that she should, at her earliest possible convenience, report to the U.S. commissioner's office in downtown Rochester. Susan, however, would not tolerate any special treatment and insisted that the marshal arrest her on the spot. She even held out her wrists and demanded to be placed in handcuffs. Obliging Susan, the marshal escorted her downtown on a horse-drawn trolley. When the conductor asked Susan for her fare, she replied that she was "traveling at the expense of the government" and told the marshal to pay.

All the women who had voted in Rochester's Eighth Ward were arrested as well (along with the young men who had registered them) and found guilty of "knowingly, wrongfully and unlawfully" voting. Bail was then set at $500 apiece. All of them paid their fines except Susan, who applied for a writ of habeas corpus. (The writ orders the police to produce

the arrested person in court.) Susan's aim in doing this was to get her case heard by the U.S. Supreme Court. When her lawyer, Henry Selden, applied for the writ, however, it was refused by the U.S. district judge in Albany, who then raised her fine to $1,000. Once again, Susan refused to pay. She said she would rather go to prison than allow the courts to block her constitutional right to vote. As Selden stood at Susan's side in the courthouse, he advised her to pay the fine and paid for it with his own money. As the two left together, Susan learned that by allowing Selden to pay her bail she had forfeited her opportunity to go before the Supreme Court. Selden told her that he could not stand to see a respected lady like Susan be put in jail. His good intentions had ruined Susan's constitutional case.

Susan's trial was set to begin on June 17, 1873. In the meantime, her speaking tour continued nonstop. She began to deliver a speech titled "Is It a Crime for Citizens of the United States to Vote?" Susan was so convincing that the prosecution became concerned they would not be able to find any neutral, open-minded jurors for their case against her. The prosecution eventually requested her trial to be moved to the U.S. circuit court in Canandaigua, New York. Susan's family arrived there just before the trial began to give her moral support. The judge assigned to the trial was Ward Hunt. Susan's case was the first he ever heard on the federal bench. Judge Hunt was eager to please his political mentor, Senator Roscoe Conkling, a die-hard opponent of woman suffrage. Unfortunately, this meant that Susan's case never had a chance. Judge Hunt did not allow her to testify in her own defense, ruling that, as a woman, she was not qualified to do so. Hunt instructed the all-male jury to find Susan guilty as charged.

Judge Hunt asked Susan if she had anything to say before he pronounced sentence. Her response would become one of the most famous speeches in the history of the women's rights movement. Susan immediately criticized him for his "high-handed" treatment during the trial. She accused him of robbing her of the fundamental privilege of citizenship. "My natural rights, my civil rights, my political rights, my judicial rights are all alike ignored," she declared. Susan went on to tell Hunt that he had "trampled under foot every vital principle of our government." Hunt repeatedly ordered Susan to stop talking and sit down, but she refused to listen. "I am degraded from the status of a citizen," she said. "Not only myself individually but all of my sex are … doomed to political subjection (control by others) under this so-called republican form of government!"

After Susan's moving speech, Judge Hunt found her guilty. He announced that Susan owed a fine of $100 and was responsible for the cost of the prosecution against her. Susan, however, had other ideas. "I will never pay a dollar of your unjust penalty!" she answered. "I shall earnestly and persistently continue to urge all women to the practical recognition of the old Revolutionary maxim, 'Resistance to tyranny is obedience to God.'" Afterward, Judge Hunt ordered Susan's release. She never did pay her fine, and the government never pursued it. Susan's trial proved to be one of the finest moments in her long career. It gave her a national platform and allowed her to describe in detail the injustice against which she was fighting. It also enabled her to express what it means to be a full citizen of the United States, with all the rights and privileges that the word implies.

Three years later, the Supreme Court effectively ruled on the matter of woman suffrage when it heard the case of *Minor v. Happersett*. In a unanimous decision, the justices ruled that citizenship meant "membership in a nation, and nothing more." They also recognized the right of each state to determine who was eligible to vote within its own borders. After conferring with Elizabeth Cady Stanton, Susan came to believe that the NWSA should pursue a different— and much more difficult—strategy. They decided that only an amendment to the U.S. Constitution would guarantee woman suffrage. This campaign would last the rest of their lives.

The Power of the Written Word

In 1876, the United States celebrated its 100th anniversary as a nation. Philadelphia, the birthplace of the Declaration of Independence, sponsored a Centennial Exhibition on Independence Day. Susan and Stanton, who felt that the women of the country had little to celebrate, decided to make their presence known. Susan was the only unmarried woman among the NWSA's leadership and so the only one able to sign a contract. She rented a place near the fairgrounds that would serve as the NWSA's headquarters. She and Stanton, along with Matilda Joslyn Gage, a writer and political activist, drew up the Declaration of Rights of the Women of the United States. It was similar in spirit to the Declaration of Rights and Sentiments that Stanton had presented to the Seneca Falls Convention in 1848. But this document was different in many of the things it called for because of the real progress Susan and Stanton had achieved over the last 25 years. For example, men were no longer seen as oppressors. It was the government, rather, that "deserved to be impeached" for preventing women from taking part as full citizens of the country. The document referred to the U.S. government as an "oligarchy of sex, and not a true republic." With this declaration in hand, Susan, Stanton, and Gage were determined for it to get a hearing at the official ceremony that was to be held in Independence Hall.

Stanton wrote to General Joseph Hawley, the president of the Centennial Commission, asking for 50 seats to be assigned to the NWSA. General Hawley, however, did not want anything to disrupt the centennial celebration and politely refused Stanton's request.

After much back and forth, though, Hawley eventually granted her four seats. Susan managed to obtain a
press pass for herself through her brother Daniel's
newspaper in Kansas. Arriving at Independence Hall
on July 4, Susan and her companions were nervous.
During the ceremony, Richard Henry Lee of Virginia,
a descendant of one of the signers of the Declaration
of Independence, began to read from the famous
document. As he spoke the words "our sacred honor,"
Susan took it as her cue and began moving down the
main aisle toward the speakers' platform with her
companions. Later, one of the witnesses would recall
that Susan had "a look of intense pain, yet historic
determination" on her face. Thomas W. Ferry, a
senator from Michigan, stood on the speakers' platform as well and was stunned to see Susan approaching. Stopping directly in front of Ferry, Susan handed
him a copy of the Declaration of Rights of the Women
of the United States. Susan and her companions began
to hand out other copies to those seated nearby. Attempting to end the disruption, General Hawley
banged his gavel and repeatedly called for order.

Susan and her companions left Independence
Hall and seized a bandstand that had been set up for a
concert that evening. Matilda Joslyn Gage held up a
parasol to protect Susan from the blistering heat of
the sun, as Susan read aloud from the Declaration of
Rights of Women to the crowd of onlookers that had
gathered around her. "We ask justice, we ask equality,"
she said. "We ask that all political and civil rights that
belong to the citizens of the United States be guaranteed to us and to our daughters forever."

Several weeks later, Susan made her way to Stanton's home in Tenafly, New Jersey. There, she and Stanton were joined by Gage and Ida Husted Harper, an author and journalist who wrote in support of women's rights. Together, the four women began work on an ambitious writing project intended to chronicle the woman suffrage movement. It was to be called the *History of Woman Suffrage*. Susan took care of the business end of the venture, finding a publisher and arranging for the book's distribution to schools and libraries. Stanton served as editor and did some of the writing. Surrounding themselves with letters and newspaper clippings, Susan and Stanton dug deep into their past, often stirring up painful memories from their long struggle to gain equality for women. Over the next decade, they produced an exhaustive record of their movement. It would eventually comprise six volumes of more than 5,700 pages. Ironically, Susan hated every minute of the work itself. She wrote in her diary that she "longed to be in the midst of the fray" and that she loved "to make history but [hated] to write it." Nevertheless, she recognized the importance of the project and her faith in it never faltered.

Building Bridges

By the 1880's, the life of the average woman in America had begun to change. Many were likely to have attended college, and many others were members of a vast array of women's clubs that had sprung up all over the country. A few of these clubs were dedicated to social reform but were overall quite conservative. Nevertheless, they encouraged women to take up leadership roles in their communities and helped support a new generation demanding to be heard. Susan had converted many of these organizations to her cause and built a powerful alliance. At the same time, she recognized that the NWSA's activities aimed at persuading the U.S. Congress to grant women the right to vote were not working. The amendment addressing woman suffrage was not even voted on by the Senate until 1887, when it lost 34 to 16.

Susan also continued to travel to build up her alliance. She even went to Europe in 1883 to lay the foundation of an international women's organization. Joining up with Stanton, who had arrived there several months earlier, Susan and two of her younger colleagues, Rachel Foster Avery and May Wright Sewall, began discussions with their European associates. The NWSA offered to host the first congress in the United States. After years of groundwork, delegates from more than 50 women's organizations

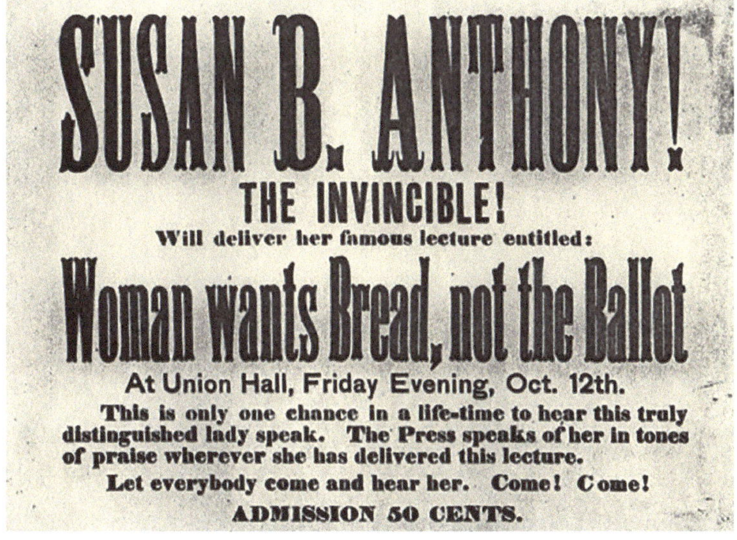

This poster advertises a lecture that Susan was scheduled to give in Boulder, Colorado, on Oct. 12, 1877. Susan traveled around the country delivering her famous lecture for several years.

across nine countries came together to form the International Council of Women (ICW). They met for the first time in Washington, D.C., on March 25, 1888. The new organization was well respected from the beginning. President Grover Cleveland even held a reception at the White House for the ICW's founding congress. At its second congress, the ICW took part in the World's Columbian Exposition. It was held in Chicago and celebrated the 400th anniversary of Columbus's voyage to America. At the last minute, it was decided that the Exposition should recognize the role of women over the last four centuries, a decision made possible by Susan's hard work behind the scenes. The

weeklong convention took place as part of the World's Columbian Exposition. It was known as the World's Congress of Representative Women. It included delegates from 27 countries and discussed the topic of woman suffrage. Susan spoke to large crowds at the Exposition and was even invited to attend Buffalo Bill Cody's Wild West Show.

Despite this international recognition, Susan knew bigger bridges would have to be built to achieve woman suffrage in the United States. She turned to her estranged friend and ally, Lucy Stone. In February 1890, after two years of careful negotiation, Susan and Stone finally agreed to join forces and merge their two organizations into the National American Woman Suffrage Association (NAWSA). Susan, Stanton, and Stone were all nominated to be president, but Stone's health was in decline and she withdrew her name from consideration. Many of the more conservative members of the NAWSA wanted Susan for the job. Though their relationship with her had been stormy in the past, they felt she could be relied on to focus on the all-important issue of woman suffrage. However, Susan hated the idea of running against Stanton. While her own fame had by now exceeded Stanton's, she urged the delegates to vote for Stanton instead of her. Stanton won, in the end, and Susan became vice president. Stone offered to serve as chairperson of the executive board. In her inaugural address, Stanton told the members of the NAWSA that they should remain open to the views of any woman who wished to speak before them. "Wherever a woman is wronged," she said, "her voice should be heard."

The following year, Susan decided to slow down, after traveling across the country and beyond for nearly half a century to spread her message. She moved in with her sister Mary, who was living at the Anthony family home in Rochester. Susan was pleased finally to have her own home, but she did not get to spend much time there. In 1892, when Stanton retired, Susan became president of the NAWSA. In 1894, New York amended its state constitution. Susan, at the age of 74, took up the challenge of visiting all of New York's counties to speak in favor of woman suffrage. When it was defeated yet again, she called it the "bitterest disappointment" of her life. However, she immediately headed west to take up the next battle. The Republicans in Kansas were going back on their word to support woman suffrage, just as they had 27 years earlier. Susan campaigned hard to prevent this, but her efforts were in vain. In 1896, Susan spent eight months campaigning in California, sometimes speaking three times a day. Unfortunately, the men of California also voted against woman suffrage.

Decades of struggle to gain woman suffrage and repeated setbacks began to take a toll on Susan. By 1900, only four states—Colorado, Idaho, Utah, and Wyoming—had granted women the right to vote. Susan spoke out against the wave of mob violence that erupted against African Americans throughout the South. She condemned the "Jim Crow" laws that attempted to reduce African Americans to second-class citizens, and she never wavered in her private views on racial equality. Nevertheless, Susan more and more bowed to pressure from the younger leaders of the NAWSA, who made it clear that African American chapters were not welcome. In 1895, she asked Frederick Douglass not to attend a convention in Atlanta, thinking that his presence would alienate white Southerners. In 1899, when the NAWSA considered publicly denouncing segregation, she failed to offer her support. The failure to win the vote for women on a national level led Susan to make choices that did not always reflect her ideals, much like her cooperation with George Francis Train years earlier.

Later Years

In 1900, at the age of 80, Susan stepped down from the presidency of the NAWSA. Among the contenders to succeed her was the Reverend Anna Howard Shaw. Shaw was one of Susan's closest friends, a fine public speaker, and a shining example of the next generation of women who were preparing to follow in Susan's footsteps. (Susan often referred to these young women leaders as her "nieces.") Another contender was Carrie Chapman Catt, whose skills at organization and

Susan (left) stepped down as head of the NAWSA in 1900 at the age of 80. She chose Anna Howard Shaw (right) as one of the people to follow in her footsteps.

Susan (standing) urged her successors in the women's rights movement to work closely together as she and Elizabeth Cady Stanton (seated) had done as leaders of the movement before them.

raising money had helped to win the vote in Colorado. Perhaps recognizing herself in Catt, Susan chose her as her successor. She urged Catt and Shaw to combine their skills and work closely together, as she and Stanton had done before them. One of Susan's longtime goals was an international organization that would reach beyond the scope of the ICW and work toward woman suffrage across the globe. In 1902, Catt organized a preliminary meeting in Washington, D.C., attended by delegates from several countries. Two years later, the International Woman Suffrage Alliance (later renamed the International Alliance of Women) was officially founded in Berlin, Germany. Susan was declared its honorary president and first member. This gave her a sense of "profound satisfaction," and she considered it the highpoint of her career.

In June 1902, Susan visited Elizabeth Cady Stanton in New York City for what would prove to be the last time. Stanton's health had been failing for some time. She was now 86 years old and had lost her eyesight. When it came time for Susan to leave, both women knew the end was near. Susan began to weep, asking, "Shall I see you again?" Keeping her composure, Stanton replied, "Oh, yes, if not here, then in the hereafter, if there is one, and if there isn't we shall never know it." Susan departed with a promise to return for Stanton's 87th birthday in November.

In October, Susan's longtime partnership with Stanton came to an end. Susan was at her home in Rochester when a messenger from Western Union came knocking at the door. (Western Union was the main provider of long-distance messages, called telegrams, sent over land wires and electric current in the United States.) Ida Husted Harper, who had become Susan's secretary and official biographer, received the telegram from Stanton's daughter, Harriot,

This image shows portraits of seven prominent women in the woman suffrage and women's rights movements, including Susan (bottom left), Lucretia Mott (top), Elizabeth Cady Stanton (top, right), Anna Dickinson (center), and others.

This photograph captures a weary-looking Susan sitting at her desk in 1905, a year before her death.

and brought it immediately to the upstairs study. Susan read the telegram in silence. It said simply, "Mother passed away at three o'clock. Harriot." Letting the telegram fall into her lap, Susan was speechless. She remained in her chair in a "melancholy quiet" for the rest of the afternoon, gazing at the portrait of Stanton hanging on the wall of the study. Harper and the other women who worked at the house left Susan alone with her grief. As the news of Stanton's death spread, the press came to the house asking for a statement. "I cannot express myself at all as I feel," Susan told them. "I am too crushed to say much, but if she had outlived me, she would have found fine words with which to express our friendship." Susan boarded a train the following day for New York City. It was a long and lonely journey.

When Susan arrived at Stanton's apartment, she was overcome by her friend's absence and her grief became more profound. The funeral was a private ceremony—at Stanton's request—with only a few friends joining the family. After the casket was closed and covered with flowers for the final services, a framed photograph of Susan was placed upon it. It was Stanton's wish to have a picture of her close friend and greatest ally with her at the end.

Despite the immeasurable loss of Elizabeth Cady Stanton, Susan continued with her work as she always had. By now, she had outlived every member of her family except her sister Mary. The younger generation was now in charge of the suffrage movement, but Susan remained a dominating presence until the end. When Carrie Chapman Catt resigned the presidency of the NAWSA in 1904 to take care of her ailing husband, Susan's influence was great enough to ensure that her second choice for the job, Anna Howard Shaw, became the next president.

After Susan suffered a stroke, her doctors suggested that she cut back on her activities. Susan, of course, would not hear of such a thing. She continued to travel, both across the United States and in Europe. Susan greatly enjoyed the near-universal affection that she now received just about everywhere she went. In February 1906, the annual convention of the NAWSA was scheduled to take place in Baltimore, Maryland. Susan was determined to go, despite experiencing shortness of breath and dizzy spells. She had missed only one meeting since the end of the Civil War. As she was leaving her home in Rochester, a blizzard descended on the city. Susan developed a cold during the journey to Baltimore. By the time she arrived in the city, she was exhausted and too weak to attend most of the sessions. However, she did not remain idle. From her sickbed, Susan managed to raise money for the suffrage movement from Johns Hopkins University and Bryn Mawr College.

"Failure Is Impossible!"

On February 15, 1906, Susan celebrated her 86th birthday. That day, she boarded a train for Washington, D.C., where friends and colleagues were holding a gathering in her honor. As usual, Susan received praise from every corner of the country, including the White House. President Theodore Roosevelt sent his "hearty good wishes for the continuation of [Susan's] useful and honorable life." Susan found his words to be empty. "I do wish men would do something besides extend congratulations," she said. "I would rather have him say a word to Congress in favor of amending the Constitution to give women suffrage."

After a day of celebration, Susan slowly made her way to the podium to thank all who had come to wish her well. She had to wait almost 10 minutes to begin, however. Giving her a standing ovation, the audience would not stop clapping for her. Anna Howard Shaw helped her stay on her feet. When she was finally able to begin, Susan seemed to grasp that this might be her last public speech. "I have looked on so many such audiences," she said, "all testifying to the righteousness, the justice, and the worthiness of the cause of woman suffrage." She spoke of her great admiration

"FAILURE IS IMPOSSIBLE"
SUSAN
B.
ANTHONY
VOTES FOR WOMEN

This ribbon, from the Brooklyn Woman Suffrage Association, honors Susan B. Anthony. The quote "Failure is impossible" is from Susan's last public speech in February 1906.

for Mary Wollstonecraft, the English writer and philosopher best known for *A Vindication of the Rights of Woman,* published in 1792. "I never met that great woman," Susan continued, "but … I have met and known most of the progressive women who came after her." Among "a long galaxy of great women," she mentioned Lucretia Mott, Lucy Stone, and Elizabeth Cady Stanton. "There have been others also just as true and devoted to the cause," she added. "I wish I could name every one—but with such women consecrating their lives, failure is impossible!"

Two days later, Susan returned to Rochester in the company of her sister Mary and her nurse. The convention had been a wonderful experience for her. But it left her feeling exhausted, and she developed a bad case of pneumonia. With her sister and Anna Howard Shaw at her bedside, Susan said, "I have been striving for a little bit of justice … and yet I must die without obtaining it. … It seems so cruel." Toward the end, as she drifted in and out of consciousness, Susan whispered the names of the many suffragists she had worked with during her long career. "I know how hard they have worked," she murmured. "I know the sacrifices they have made." On March 13, 1906, Susan B. Anthony died. Her death was widely mourned. Upon hearing the sad news, Clara Barton, the founder of the American Red Cross, predicted that full equality for women, thanks to Susan's lifelong efforts, was "not far away."

Susan's funeral took place at the Central Presbyterian Church in Rochester. Twelve women dressed in white formed a guard around her simple Quaker casket as 10,000 mourners passed by. Susan was dressed in her traditional black-silk gown with an American flag pin on her breast. It had four tiny diamonds that represented the states that had given women the right to vote. After the mourners passed by, the pin was given to Anna Howard Shaw and the casket was closed. In solemn procession, those who had come to pay their final respects to Susan filed out of the church. More than 25,000 people, many who could not get in the church, made their way to the cemetery where Susan's parents were buried. Susan was laid to rest alongside them. Anna Howard Shaw spoke eloquently in praise of her mentor: "There is no death for such as she. There are no last words of love. … Her work will not be finished, nor will her last word be spoken, while there remains a wrong to be righted or a fettered life to be freed in all the earth."

Three women pose in front of a horse-drawn wagon with a sign on it saying the National American Woman Suffrage Association supports a resolution drafted by Susan B. Anthony.

In 1979 and 1980, the U.S. government minted for circulation a $1 coin bearing Susan B. Anthony's likeness. She was the first woman to be pictured on a United States coin in general circulation.

Born under the most ordinary of circumstances, Susan B. Anthony rose to become one of the most unconventional women of the 1800's. Of all the women who fought for equality at a time when such a thing seemed impossible, Susan's career was perhaps the most dramatic, her personality the most charismatic. She was certainly the movement's most capable organizer. Though she did not live to see it, her struggle for woman suffrage was eventually won, 14 years after her death. In 1920, the Nineteenth Amendment to the United States Constitution, popularly known as the "Anthony Amendment," was finally adopted and gave women in the United States the right to vote. After its ratification, the NAWSA was transformed into the League of Women Voters, an organization that remains a powerful force in American politics.

Today, Susan B. Anthony is considered the "Mother of Us All" by many feminists and finds her place among those who fought for racial justice in America. Early in her career, she traveled across New York and New England to condemn the great injustice of slavery, while at the same time fighting for the cause of women. In the years leading up to the 1900's, she fought to ensure the rights of the former enslaved people who had won their freedom during the Civil War, and she worked toward achieving woman suffrage. Though she was by no means perfect, Susan B. Anthony never wavered in her struggle to gain equal rights for all Americans. She is remembered as a tireless champion of justice and equality.

INDEX

FURTHER READING

Hull, N. E. H. *The Woman Who Dared to Vote: The Trial of Susan B. Anthony.* Univ. Pr. of Kans., 2012.

National Susan B. Anthony Museum & House. https://susanbanthonyhouse.org/

Todd, Anne M. *Susan B. Anthony, Activist.* Chelsea Hse., 2009.

ACKNOWLEDGMENTS

Cover: © PhotoQuest/Getty Images

3 Public Domain

7-10 Library of Congress

12 © DeAgostini/Getty Images

15-16 Public Domain

18 Library of Congress

23-24 Public Domain

25 © Corbis/VCG/Getty Images

27 Library of Congress

28 © Corbis/VCG/Getty Images

31-32 Library of Congress

35 Public Domain

37 © Bettmann/Getty Images

40 National Portrait Gallery, Smithsonian Institution

43-45 Library Of Congress

49 National Archives

50 © Eon Images

55-80 Library of Congress

83 © Hulton Archive/Getty Images

84-90 Library of Congress

91 © Everett Historical/Shutterstock

92 © Daniel D Malone, Shutterstock